My Favourite
Prayers

My Favourite Prayers

Selwyn Hughes

My Favourite Prayers by Selwyn Hughes

Copyright © Selwyn Hughes 2001

Published by CWR, Waverley Abbey House, Waverley Lane, Farnham, Surrey, GU9 8EP.

ISBN 1-85345-195-9
All Scripture quotations in this publication are taken from the Holy Bible, New International Version (NIV). Copyright © 1973, 1978, 1984, International Bible Society. Used by permission.

Concept development, editing, design and production by CWR. Cover image: Photodisc. Internal images: Eyewire.

Printed by Cox and Wyman

Contents

Introduction

Prayer is an intimate place where we meet with God and share our hearts. It is an opportunity for us to communicate with our Creator and to see Him at work in our lives. As Robert Moffatt writes: "Prayer is love in need appealing to love in power."

I hope the prayers in this book help you to find the words that often get lost when we find ourselves submerged by circumstances.

Selwyn Hughes

The author's royalties from this book will be donated to a selection of Children's charities throughout the world.

1

Relationship with GOD

Seeking to Know GOD

O God, hidden and yet right here, I seek after You. I know You exist and I so want come to terms with You. I am eager to know You personally. Please reveal Yourself to me through Your Son Jesus Christ.

As I reach up to You, reach down to me, I pray. Come and save me. Forgive my sins, assure me of Your gift of salvation. In Christ's Name I ask it.

Amen.

Beginning a
NEW *Day*

Lord Jesus Christ, You are my centre and my focus. You know every step I will take this day, every thought that will arise in my mind, every person I will meet.

Help me to be Your ambassador so that, in everything I do and everywhere I go, I will be a true witness of Your love and saving grace. For Your own dear Name's sake I ask it.

Amen.

Feeling Spiritually COLD

Father, I am conscious that things are not as they were between us. My heart is growing cold, my life lacks the spiritual energy I once had. I repent of my growing indifference.

Help me, and help me now, to return to the passion of my first love. Breathe on the dying embers of my heart until they burst once more into flame. For Jesus' sake.

Amen.

Lacking Spiritual POWER

Lord Jesus Christ, I know that
Your distinctive baptism brings with it
the power of Your Holy Spirit. I need
that power today; I need that inner
reinforcement.

Spirit of God, descend upon my
heart right now as I wait before You.
Change the whole focus of my life. Make
me full and running over. In Your Name
I ask it.

Amen.

Seeking DIVINE *Guidance*

Father God, I want to know Your will and to follow it daily. If you have any word to speak to me today, through the Scriptures, through others, or by Your voice in my own heart, let me hear that word and follow it.

I submit my will to Your will, my way to Your way. Guide me, heavenly Father. In Jesus' Name.

Amen.

Failure to GROW

O God, help me understand that I am made to grow spiritually and, when I am not growing, I do not fulfil the purpose of my being.

You have provided everything for my growth through prayer, the Scriptures, and the empowerment of the Holy Spirit. Teach me how to possess my possessions. I yield my all to You. Make me a growing Christian. In Jesus' Name.

Amen.

DESIRING *a* Deeper Prayer Life

O God, forgive me that so often I fail to pray the way I ought. Give me greater power and prowess in prayer.

Search me and see if there are any hidden ways in me, then teach me how to pray. I want to emerge from the prayer moment more alive and closer to You. Help me see prayer as a priority.

Amen.

YEARNING *for God's Holy Spirit*

My God, I want to know the continuing fullness of Your Holy Spirit. I want the Spirit who creates a passion for souls and sacrifice to hold perpetual sway over my whole being.

Give me that constant empowering that never tires or flags. Fill me so full of Your Self that I may shed all self-conscious fear and stand up, as Your effective servant. In Jesus' Name.

Amen.

Seeking a Spiritual CHALLENGE

O God my Father, give me spiritual tasks to do for You that are beyond me, so that I have to draw heavily upon Your resources. Help me not to limit myself to things I can already do easily, as this will not stretch me.

I ask not for tasks suitable to my powers, but powers suitable to my tasks. Stretch me, dear Lord, for Your praise and glory.

Amen.

2

Feeling DISCOURAGED

When Fears
INVADE

Father, I know You have fashioned me for faith and confidence. Forgive me that I have allowed fear to invade me. I know that faith is of You and fear is not of You.

I come now and lay all my fears at your feet. Let Your Love flow in, for when Love flows in, fear flows out. I open my heart to that Love right now. Flow into my life, dear Father. In Jesus' Name.

Amen.

Lacking COURAGE

Lord Jesus Christ, You who faced everything that came Your way with quiet confidence and courage, help me catch that same spirit as I face what lies ahead of me now. Help me know that Your will underpins my will, Your adequacy supports my inadequacy.

I throw open every pore of my being to Your strength and power. In You I am more than a match for anything. Thank You, Father. In Jesus' Name.

Amen.

Power to do the RIGHT THING

God my Father, give me courage and power to do the right thing. If ever I needed Your grace, it is now. I am facing something that is beyond my strength so I draw instead on Yours. I know You will not fail me. So I rise to go forward in Your Name. Together we march to victory.

Amen.

Feeling INADEQUATE *to the task*

Father, You are life's supreme affirmation. You are sufficient and you are power. I throw open every aspect of my being to you, to let you come in and change me from being efficient to being effective; from feeling inadequate to becoming adequate through You.

I take on your power for the task that is ahead. With You all things are possible. I am so thankful.

Amen.

DISCOURAGED *by the Standards of the World*

O God, I live in an age when the ropes that held our civilisation together are becoming frayed. Standards are falling and it seems that anything goes.

Help me not to surrender my standards in the light of what I see around me. Help me to be different, but not arrogant or superior, just different – so that the people I meet might see You in me. In Jesus' Name.

Amen

3

Fear and TURMOIL

DAUNTED *by*
the Day Ahead

Heavenly Father, lead me in
triumph through this day, for there are
situations I must face that I fear will sap
my natural strength. May I meet all
things not in my strength but in Yours.

Empower me so that I may meet
all hate with Your love, all indifference
with Your interest, all resistance with
Your compassion. In Jesus' Name.

Amen.

WORRIED
about Today

Father, help me realise that
nothing can happen today that You and I
can't handle together. I am weak and can
take only a small part of the load – You
will have to take the heavy end.

Please take my hand in Yours. Let's
walk together into the day. You have my
will and I have Your power. This is
going to be a great day. In Jesus' Name.

Amen.

CONCERNED
about Tomorrow

O God, forgive me. Why do I needlessly burden myself about tomorrow when Your grace is given only for the present moment?

Whatever happens tomorrow, and however heavy the load, You will help me carry it. I only add to my burdens and diminish my strength to deal with the affairs of today when I worry about tomorrow. You are in all my tomorrows as You are in all my todays. My trust is in You.

Amen.

Fear of CHANGE

Father, help me, with good grace, to accept the changes I can do nothing about. Grant that no change shall disturb me on the inside, no matter how many there are on the outside.

No change can disturb this perfect peace which You have created in my soul. So, whatever changes may come, help me hold on to You, the changeless One.

Amen.

Afraid of
GROWING OLD

O God, help me grow old gracefully, beautifully and creatively. Keep me active and give me the strength and will to bring forth fruit, even to old age. May I greet the advancing years not with a sigh but with a song. For in You I have not just life, but a deathless life. I am deeply grateful.

Amen.

AFRAID *to Die*

Lord Jesus Christ, I am grateful for the victory You accomplished when You rose from the dead. Now that victory is mine. Death may come to my body but it can never affect my soul. I am bound for eternity.

Take away all fear of dying from my heart and burn this truth within me. I live in a resurrected Christ, since He cannot die, neither can I.

Amen.

FACING
Middle Age

My Father and my God, I am now in the time of life where changes in my body are beginning to affect me in my inner life, particularly my attitudes and my thoughts. Yet, as I grow older, I am gathering experience – help me make that larger experience work for me and for You in ways that contribute to my life and also to Your kingdom. In Jesus' Name.

Amen.

Worried about GROWING OLDER

O God, my physical powers are no longer what they used to be, but Your touch can not only sustain them but heighten them. Touch me and strengthen me, so that every day I may be alert and ready to do whatever You want me to do. Give me the strength to bring forth fruit, even into old age. In Jesus' Name.

Amen.

4

Sickness and HEALING

Sick and AFFLICTED

Loving heavenly Father, multitudes of Your children have been touched and healed by You. Now I am in the same need.

Stretch forth Your healing hand and place it upon my body. Heal my sickness and restore me to health. Show me if there is anything in me hindering my healing – resentment, jealousy, or any other thing. Reveal it to me and I will deal with it. Then restore me to health, dear Lord. In Jesus' Name.

Amen.

BURNT *Out*

My Father and my God, I have burned up my soul and body in my effort to get through the days. Such tension has taken me nowhere, except deeper into the mire.

Help me, this day and every day, to link all my energies to the calm of Your purposes. Breathe Your peace and calmness into my restless spirit. For Jesus' sake.

Amen.

Under Constant PRESSURE

O living healing Christ, I come to You seeking rest for my soul. I want the roots of my weariness to be removed. If they have been covered up by excuses and rationalisations, then help me right now to uncover them. I want to be whole – perfectly whole. Grant me this favour for Your own dear Name's sake.

Amen.

5

Family and RELATIONSHIPS

A CRITICAL *Spirit*

O God, You who judge me lovingly, help me judge others in the same way. Help me to be more creative than critical and, where possible, help others overcome their difficulties rather than condemn them. Help me see the good, not just the bad. And help me not to be glad when others go wrong. In Jesus' Name.

Amen.

Finding it
HARD *to Love*

O Father, I know Your way is the
way of love, and You have created us to
embody this love. But sometimes this is
not so easy. My carnal nature rises up to
drown the love You have put in my
heart. Help me turn the tables on this
situation and let Your love flow through
me to others, especially those who are
difficult to love. In Jesus' Name.

Amen.

A HEART FILLED
with Hate

O Father, this fire of hate that is within my heart is consuming me. It is consuming everything noble within me. Quench its fire now. Let no smouldering embers remain.

I consent for the last spark of hate to be put out and replaced with kindness toward others. Help me understand that I cannot hurt another person without hurting you. In Jesus' Name.

Amen.

Family PRESSURES

Dear Father, You who have set us in families as a training ground for living together harmoniously, give me the wisdom and power I need to play my part in my family. If there are changes needed, begin with me. Make me a true ambassador of Your grace and my home an embassy of heaven. In Jesus' Name.
Amen.

Being a GOOD *Influence at Home*

Heavenly Father, help me bring into my home such a flame of pure living that others may catch from me a fire that will never go out. You gave Your disciples power in the very place they had failed – Jerusalem. Give me this power where I am likely to fail most – in the home. For Jesus' sake.

Amen.

DIVIDED *Loyalties*

Father, you said a house divided against itself cannot stand. Help me to be a more single-minded person. Your Son's single-minded devotion to Your will is an example I want to follow. I want to be unanimous from this hour and the chaos of inner division replaced with singleness of purpose. May all clamouring voices be stilled at the voice of Your command. Don't let me waver, let me win. In Christ's Name.

Amen.

A Need for
RECONCILIATION

O God, you are the great reconciler. Give me Your Spirit as I set about this task. Sensitive emotions are at stake and my attempt at reconciliation might be rejected. My choice of words is important in this task. Help me, my Father. Hold me fast, but help me to do the right thing, even though my efforts may come to naught. In Jesus' Name.

Amen.

Being INSENSITIVE *to Others*

Lord Jesus Christ, You who cared for those who hammered You to the cross and said, "Forgive them for they know not what they do," help me to care like that.

My love is so limited, so narrow, so parochial. I bring my limited love to Your limitless love. Pour into me Your love until it overflows to others.

Amen.

NEW *Relationships*

Father God, I know no relationship can remain outside Your sway. Guide me so that this relationship will be glorifying to You. If it is Your will that it develops, then help me to take it at Your pace, not mine.

No matter what happens, grant that no earthly relationship will ever displace my relationship with You. In Jesus' Name.

Amen.

A Friend in NEED

O God, You who have been a rock beneath my feet, help me to be a rock to the one I love who is in trouble at this time. Show me how to pray and to minister to them so that the sinking sands might turn to rock. Use me as You have never used me before, I pray in Jesus' Name.

Amen.

6

Sin and REPENTANCE

Caught up in SELFISH PURSUITS

O Father, forgive me for thinking more of myself than I ought. You delivered me from the dominance of myself, but here I am caught up in the futility of a self-centred life.

Help me to be more loving, thinking of You and others. Then life will catch a new freshness and flavour. I turn right now from self-centredness towards benevolence. Give me grace to be all You want me to be. In Jesus' Name.

Amen.

Full of SELF-PITY

O God, forgive me for whining at life and consoling myself with a panacea like "poor me" or "Why should this happen to me?" Help me see that these are just pathetic attempts to deal with my disappointments and hurt, instead of putting my trust in You.

As I reach up now to You, lift my feet out of the quicksand of self-pity. Release me and set me free. In Jesus' Name.

Amen.

FILLED *with* *Self-hate*

O God, You Whose love is constant despite my imperfections, help me develop that same kind of love towards myself. Bring me to a place where I can dislike those parts of me that need perfecting without rejecting the rest of my personality.

You believe in me, no matter what. Help me believe in myself. In Jesus' Name.

Amen.

REPENTANCE
of Sin

O God, I come to You in deep repentance and contrition. I carry this inner hell within me, but now I turn it over to You. Forgive me for my sin, cleanse me by Your blood and bury it at the foot of Your cross.

I belong to heaven, not hell. Release me and forgive me. In Christ's Name I receive that forgiveness. Thank You, my Father. Help me show my gratitude in a new way of living.

Amen.

FALLEN
from Grace

Heavenly Father, I come to You with my wayward will. I have gone astray because I wanted my own way more than Yours. Forgive me and restore me dear Father.

I come to You with a humbled heart, humbled through my sin and my failure. But now I am wiser. My hope in the future is to keep close to You. Draw me closer and keep me ever at Your side. In Jesus' Name.

Amen.

TROUBLED *by* *Evil Thoughts*

Lord Jesus Christ, no evil thought could live in Your mind, for purity gave no place to evil. Fill my mind with Your purity and Your power so that evil thoughts will find no place in me either. I know You will do Your part; help me do mine by filling my mind with thoughts of You and the principles that come from Your Word. For Your own dear Name's sake.

Amen.

STRUGGLING *with Sexual Desires*

Father, I am getting lost in this jungle of sexual desire and day by day it grows more tangled. I need wisdom and I need power, for this lust is clamorous and often drowns out Your still small voice.

I bring my sex drive and lay it on the altar of Your love. We must work this out together. Quiet my thoughts and direct them by Your will. In Jesus' Name I ask it.

Amen.

Wanting to Run from REALITY

O Father, part of Your salvation is to help me face reality, not to run away from it. All evasions of reality, all subterfuges, are really a lack of trust – trust in You. Help me catch the quiet courage of Your Son who faced everything, knowing You were with Him and would not forsake Him. In His peerless and precious name I pray.

Amen.

Thinking of Tomorrow to AVOID TODAY

O God my Father, I know I must consider and think of the future, but not as a means of overlooking the present. Yesterday is history, tomorrow a dream, today is reality. Help me to face the issues that confront me today and bring out of this day Your best and my best. In Jesus' Name.

Amen.

When BIGOTRY Drives Out Love

My God, help me to see that You are a Father, not just to me, but to all Your children. Forgive me for loving selectively, instead of fully. Deepen my understanding of the fact that I cannot get along with myself without getting along with the rest of Your family. I must live by love or else I live by loss. Help me live by love – love for everyone. In Jesus' Name.

Amen.

7

Bondage and OBSTACLES

Seeking DELIVERANCE *from Sinful Habits*

O God, You who sent Your Son into this world to set men and women free, I surrender into Your hands today this habit that is holding me in bondage. I cannot seem to break it but I am willing for You to break it.

Deliver me from it and set me free. I rise up now, strong in Your strength, to throw off this foreign yoke.

Amen, and Amen.

In BONDAGE *to* Material Things

Father, I am aware that material things are not an enemy to be fought but an ally to be sought. Set me free from the terrible attachment to things, I pray. Let things be, not my master, but my servant, to be used for Your praise and glory.

May I always live under Your guidance and help me understand that I am a steward of the things in my possession, not the proprietor.

Amen.

BOUND *by* *Inhibitions*

O Father, I pray that You will loose me from all the inhibitions that prevent me from being my best for You. These fetters have held me too long.

Now I want to be free to be the person You want me to be. Make me a more outgoing person, one who breaks through natural inhibitions to give myself to others. In Jesus' Name I pray. *Amen.*

THROWING OFF
the Shackles
that Bind

Father, You have told me in Your
Word to throw off every weight that
hinders for, in the race that I have to
run, nothing must hamper my progress.
Help me this day to let go every weight
that might slow down my pace, for I
would be spiritually fit and prepared for
what lies ahead. In Jesus' Name I ask it.

Amen.

Blocked by CIRCUMSTANCE

O Father, help me see that it is not so much what happens to me but my reaction to it that is important. Help me understand that You can turn all blocks into blessings, all setbacks into springboards, and all stumbling blocks into stepping stones. All things serve me when I am Yours. Thank You, my Father.

Amen.

8

HURT *and*
Disappointment

LET DOWN
by Others

My Saviour and my God, I am so thankful that I can hold onto my faith in You when others fail me. Help me not to allow my disappointments to sour me against people or hold in my heart any lingering resentment. Perhaps I wouldn't be hurt so much if I depended more on You and less on others. Help me, dear Saviour.

Amen.

RETURNING
from Failure

Father, I accept that what has happened has happened and, by Your strength and grace, I will now work with You to make the best of this failure.

No failure is failure if it succeeds in driving me to Your side. I come to You not only to lean on You, but to ask Your help in learning what I need to learn from this failure. Give me Your wisdom and set me on my feet again. In Jesus' Name.

Amen.

DISILLUSIONED
and in Despair

O God, my Father, how often I have sought to resolve my disillusionment and despair through means other than You. Forgive me for this. Now I bring all my troubles and place them at Your feet, for I know You are the Answer.

Help me, I pray, in my hour of need. To whom else can I go? Only You can keep my heart in confidence and peace. In Jesus' Name.

Amen.

HURT *by an Insult*

Lord Jesus Christ, You took all insults into Your heart and emerged from them with poise and power. Help me do the same. Words hurt, but I come to You now, the One Who specialises in healing hurts.

Put Your balm into my wounded spirit and heal me, so that I can go on without lingering bitterness or resentment. Thank You, my Saviour, for I know the work is being done.

Amen.

GRIEVING
Over a Loved One

My Father and my God, You who knows what it is to lose a Son. Help me now in my hour of grief for my loved one. I don't want to get over this but through it. I would not escape the pain but I want You to come into it. I know that, for some, grief sours rather than sweetens. Grant me Your grace so that my spirit will not be soured. In Jesus' Name I ask it.

Amen.

DISTRESSED *by World Events*

Father, as I look around I see so many things being shaken, help me never to forget that I belong to an unshakeable kingdom. I may shake on this rock but the Rock never shakes beneath me.

Deepen the assurance within me that, no matter what happens around me, Your purposes will never be derailed. I am so thankful. Blessed be Your Name forever.

Amen.

A JOYLESS *Soul*

Father, You have given me the task of spreading joy, yet how can I when joy seems to have fled my own heart?

Help me find the cause for this. Perhaps it is some moral lapse, some unconfessed sin. Show me what it is, dear Lord, so that I can put it right and have joy fill and flood my heart once again. In Jesus' Name.

Amen.

Feeling LONELY

O Father, I know I have Your friendship and companionship, but I long for human companionship also. However, in my loneliness, help me not to succumb to self-pity. Help me to examine my heart and see if there are things in me, such as shyness or pride, that tend to hinder other people's advances towards me.

I know that, to have a friend, I need to be a friend. Draw close to me and show me what I should do. In Jesus' Name.

Amen.

RESENTMENT

Father, I know that I cannot wrong another without hurting myself. This fire of resentment that burns inside me is consuming everything fine and noble that You have built into me.

Quench the fires of resentment inside me now, today. Let no smouldering ember remain. I consent for the very last spark to be put out. In Christ's Name.

Amen.

WRONGED
by Another

O God, this wrong has entered deep into my spirit and I am feeling bitterly hurt. I lay this hurt at Your feet and I ask that Your healing balm might cure the soreness within my soul. Grant that no lingering bitterness shall stay within me, for life is too short to remain bitter.

Your Son forgave even those who were crucifying Him. Help me offer forgiveness to those who have wronged me. In Jesus' Name.

Amen.

A JEALOUS
Heart

Lord Jesus Christ, save me from comparing myself with others – the root of jealousy – and teach me how to compare myself only with You. Help me rejoice in the joy of all Your children, to feel success in the success of everyone who is Your child.

Infuse me with Your Spirit so that I love everyone with a creative love. For Your own dear Name's sake.

Amen.

Holding a GRUDGE

Father, help me see that a heart
that holds a grudge inside holds a part
of hell within it. I consent for the poison
to be removed – now. Help me
understand why I might be holding it,
perhaps for the feeling of power it gives
me to hold something against someone.
To give it up renders me powerless, but I
will do it anyway. For Your sake.

Amen.

9

Disobedience and
REBELLION

Lacking in DISCIPLINE

Lord Jesus Christ, You who were so disciplined yet so free, teach me the secret. I know that it is only as I am disciplined that I can develop.

Father, teach me to take care, day by day, of the little things that need to be done; only then I will be ready to deal with the bigger issues. Give me that gentle courage that will enable me to face life thoughtfully and with unwavering persistence.

Amen.

EXPERIENCING
God's Discipline

Father, Your discipline is strict and
demanding, but the end is redemption.
Help me not to chafe at the discipline I
am going through at this moment, but to
accept it as a token, not of Your anger,
but of Your love.

You love me as I am, but You love
me too much to let me stay as I am.
Help me understand that all Your laws
are love. In Jesus' Name.

Amen.

STRUGGLING
Against God's Will

Father I know that You have fashioned my inner being for Your will, but sometimes there rises up within me a desire to make my own way rather than take Yours.

Lord, help me relate to Your will for me rather than my own, and help me understand, even more deeply, that You always give the best to those who leave the choice to You. In Jesus' Name.

Amen.

NO TIME *for*
Daily Devotions

O God, help me realise that a daily intake from You, through prayer and the reading of Your Word, is as necessary as regular food. If every time I missed an appointment with You I were to miss a meal, the lesson would soon get home to my soul.

I commit myself now to spending time with You daily. You keep Your word to me; help me keep my word to You.

Amen.

COMPROMISING
Biblical Standards

O Father, give me the power to stand up for what I believe, without compromise. It is so easy to rationalise issues, but help me to be clear on biblical standards and stick to them, come what may. Help me to do this with humility and without arrogance.

I want people to see Jesus in all I do. Grant that it may be so. In His peerless and precious Name I pray.

Amen.

10

Burdens and
PRESSURES

Too BUSY *for God*

Lord Jesus Christ, teach me how to discern between the urgent and the important. I have time enough for everything You want me to do.

Help me understand that time management is really self-management. Perhaps I get drawn into too many things. Help me, my Father, to avoid the tyranny of the urgent. In Jesus' Name.

Amen.

Establishing PRIORITIES

Lord Jesus Christ, You called Your disciples to rest from the many things that clutter up life; now help me recognise this call to my own heart and be glad to spend time with You in spiritual retreat.

You call me to Your side to rest, and not just rest, but learn how to let go of some things in order to do the more important things well. Help me my Saviour to learn this art.

Amen.

When BOREDOM *Sets In*

O Father, can this boredom come from the fact that I am more taken up with myself than I am with others? Can it be that, although I am a Christian, I am more concerned about what I can get than what I can give? Forgive me if this is so.

Cleanse me and give me a new sense of purpose – a purpose that takes me beyond myself. In Jesus' Name.

Amen.

Coping with a DISABILITY

Father, help me understand that what I lack in nature I can make up by grace. I cannot draw heavily on many physical things but I can draw heavily on You. Help me, by Your grace, to make my handicaps Your handiwork.

Let my focus be not on what I do not have, but on what I do have. I have You, and with You all things serve.

Amen.

Feeling Life is FRUITLESS

Heavenly Father, I know that every branch in You that bears fruit is pruned by You, so that it can produce more fruit.

Prune me so that I might be more fruitful and bring the greatest glory to Your name. Help me not to resist Your cuts, for this is what the pruning process demands. I am Yours to do with whatever You will.

Amen.

11

Praise and THANKS

Receiving a Special BLESSING

Thank You, my Father, for what You have done for me. O for a thousand tongues to sing my great Redeemer's praise. Help me express my gratitude, not only in ecstatic praise but in quiet ways of helpfulness to others. Help me to help the next person I meet who is in need. For Jesus' sake.

Amen.

Blessed by a New REVELATION

Gracious God, how can I ever thank You sufficiently for revealing to me new truths from Your Word. Constant surprises come to me from your Holy Scriptures. Help me never take them for granted but to take them with gratitude.

My soul is alive with expectation. May new meanings unfold. Help me behold ever more new and wondrous truths from Your Word.

Amen.

When Blessed by or THROUGH OTHERS

Father, I see that everything comes from You, but some of this "everything" comes through others. I am grateful for all that comes from You, but help me to be grateful also to the one through whom it comes.

I take from You with both hands, but teach me how to take from others with at least one hand. In Jesus' Name. *Amen.*

Praise for the
GIFT OF JOY

Father, thank you for the gift of
Your incorruptible joy – a joy that does
not depend on circumstances and does
not fade. Yours is a joy that sustains me
even when I do not feel like laughing.
Blessed be Your Name forever.

Amen

Praise for
GOD'S PATIENCE

Heavenly Father, I am so thankful that Your patience and persistence have made me what I am today. Help me deal with others in the same redemptive and patient way.

Amen

Blessed by the CREATOR

My God, my Father, how can I
ever begin to thank You enough for
designing me in this wonderful way?
The more praise I give to You O Lord,
the more I find I have to express. This
cycle of praise to You will never end.
Praise Your wonderful Name.

Amen

Blessed by
KNOWING GOD

O Father, I am so grateful that You make our relationship possible. I thought maturity was going to be a long, uphill struggle, but now I see it grows out of my relationship with You. Help me to open every pore of my being to Your endless, undying love. In Christ's Precious Name.

Amen

Blessed by
THE CHURCH

O Jesus Saviour, I am so grateful that I am here in this time and place and that I am also part of something that has an eternal existence. Church buildings can be easily knocked down and destroyed, but never Your Church. This will stand throughout eternity.

Amen

NATIONAL DISTRIBUTORS

UK: (AND COUNTRIES NOT LISTED BELOW)
CWR, PO Box 230, Farnham, Surrey GU9 8EP.
Tel: (01252) 784710 Outside UK (44) 1252 784710

AUSTRALIA: CMC Australasia, PO Box 519, Belmont, Victoria 3216. Tel: (03) 5241 3288

CANADA: CMC Distribution Ltd, PO Box 7000, Niagara on the Lake, Ontario L0S 1J0. Tel: (0800) 325 1297

GHANA: Challenge Enterprises of Ghana, PO Box 5723, Accra. Tel: (021) 222437/223249 Fax: (021) 226227

HONG KONG: Cross Communications Ltd, 1/F, 562A Nathan Road, Kowloon. Tel: 2780 1188 Fax: 2770 6229

INDIA: Crystal Communications, 10-3-18/4/1, East Marredpally, Secunderabad – 500 026. Tel/Fax: (040) 7732801

KENYA: Keswick Bookshop, PO Box 10242, Nairobi. Tel: (02) 331692/226047

MALAYSIA: Salvation Book Centre (M) Sdn Bhd, 23 Jalan SS 2/64, 47300 Petaling Jaya, Selangor. Tel: (03) 78766411/78766797 Fax: (03) 78757066/78756360

NEW ZEALAND: CMC New Zealand Ltd, Private Bag, 17910 Green Lane, Auckland. Tel: (09) 5249393 Fax: (09) 5222137

NIGERIA: FBFM, Helen Baugh House, 96 St Finbarr's College Road, Akoka, Lagos. Tel: (01) 7747429/4700218/825775/827264

PHILIPPINES: OMF Literature Inc, 776 Boni Avenue, Mandaluyong City. Tel: (02) 531 2183 Fax: (02) 531 1960

REPUBLIC OF IRELAND: Scripture Union, 40 Talbot Street, Dublin 1. Tel: (01) 8363764

SINGAPORE: Campus Crusade Asia Ltd, 315 Outram Road, 06-08 Tan Boon Liat Building, Singapore 169074. Tel: (065) 222 3640

SOUTH AFRICA: Struik Christian Books, 80 MacKenzie Street, PO Box 1144, Cape Town 8000. Tel: (021) 462 4360 Fax: (021) 461 3612

SRI LANKA: Christombu Books, 27 Hospital Street, Colombo 1. Tel: (01) 433142/328909

TANZANIA: CLC Christian Book Centre, PO Box 1384, Mkwepu Street, Dar es Salaam. Tel: (051) 2119439

UGANDA: New Day Bookshop, PO Box 2021, Kampala. Tel: (041) 255377

ZIMBABWE: Word of Life Books, Shop 4, Memorial Building, 35 S Machel Avenue, Harare. Tel: (04) 781305 Fax: (04) 774739

For e-mail addresses, visit the CWR web site: www.cwr.org.uk

My Favourite
£3.99

My Favourite Stories about Children
These charming stories about things that children say and do will amuse and delight your friends and your congregation. A wonderful book that will make you smile and remind you what a blessing children really are.

My Favourite Quotes and Anecdotes
An amusing book of stories that work as well at the dinner table or party as they do in the pulpit or the boardroom. A great gift for young and old alike and a helpful aid to anyone involved in public speaking.

Tails

Devotional Activity Books: £3.95
Story Books: £4.95

Tails is an exciting series created to help young children understand the Bible. The books are written by the award winning children's author, **Karyn Henley**, and the characters are created by **Debbie Smith** who works with the Oscar winning **Wallace and Gromit**™ team.

Devotional Activity Books
Bible Friends
Learn about great Bible friendships such as Jonathan and David and Mary and Martha.

Who is Jesus?
Discover the One who is the Son of God, the Prince of Peace, the Friend and Helper.

Let's Worship
Learn to worship anytime and anywhere, alone or with others.

Story Books
Friends Forever
No matter how many mistakes we make true friends always love us.

Who's Whoo-oo-oo?
Jesus is revealed as our best Friend.

Twigs and the Treasure Box
Tails friends discover the greatest treasure of all.

One-Year devotionals

This attractive series features easy to read selections from Selwyn Hughes' most popular work, **Every Day with Jesus**. The luxurious presentation of these pocket-sized books makes them an inspired gift or travel companion.

Meeting with God

Living with Jesus

Walking in the Spirit

Pocket Encouragers
£3.99

This new series offers biblical help, guidance and encouragement. Each title explores various aspects of the Christian experience, such as relationships, Bible study and coping with responsibility. Some content is common to all titles, with unique material that relates especially to men, women, leaders or young adults. Great gifts!

Pocket Encourager for Men

Pocket Encourager for Women

Pocket Encourager for Leaders

Pocket Encourager for Young Adults

Help
Help
Any one there
A MEN